RAIN FOREST

Linking Environmental Studies
With Everyday Life

by Shirley Cook

Incentive Publications, Inc.
Nashville, Tennessee

Illustrated by Marta Drayton
Cover by Wendi Powell
Edited by Leslie Britt

ISBN 0-86530-275-8

Table of Contents

PREFACE

Our world is becoming smaller. No longer are we divided by bodies of water, or mountain ranges, or invisible political boundaries. With inventions such as the television, the telephone, and the radio, modern technology has brought all people closer together. We are not members of separate nations, but are all united as the inhabitants of Planet Earth. As such, we are jointly responsible for one another's welfare and for the health of our planet. Keeping our planet and its people safe and healthy is a job for all cultures and all nations. The air we breathe, the water we drink, the land we plow, and the sky we gaze upon have become common ground for a world of caretakers. One nation's irresponsible actions can, indeed, affect the quality of life in other corners of the Earth.

Rain Forest is designed to help children "connect" with another environment by illuminating our ties to the tropical rain forests of the world. Children will study the plant life, animal life, and indigenous peoples of these forests by taking an alphabetical journey through this most breathtaking part of the Earth.

For each area of the rain forest that is examined, activities which require higher-level thinking strategies and which connect all areas of the curriculum are offered. Background information is provided for teachers and students. Activities have been categorized according to level of difficulty: Primary activities are, of course, less challenging than Intermediate activities. Research activities designed to enhance each area of study are designated "Questions Worth Researching." These questions are also categorized according to level of difficulty. This format will accommodate a wide range of abilities and age groups. Teachers will be able to pick and choose the activities and research tasks which are valid for their individual groups of students.

Rain Forest will help students understand that caring for Planet Earth is everyone's job and that we are all brothers and sisters in this important work—regardless of our cultural or geographical differences.

ANIMALS

BACKGROUND

About fifty percent of the world's animal species make their homes in the rain forest. Some of these species require such specialized habitats that they are not able to exist outside of this environment. As forested land is cleared, certain species have become endangered or extinct. Those animals most seriously affected by habitat destruction are the "endemic" species (species found in only one area), for if their habitat is disturbed, the species may become extinct.

To give you a better idea of the large numbers of species found in the rain forest, consider this information. In an area of about four square miles of rain forest, the following estimated numbers of living things could be found:

1. 400 species of birds
2. 150 species of butterflies
3. 100 species of reptiles
4. 125 species of mammals
5. 60 species of amphibians
6. 40,000 species of insects.

Scientists estimate that 100 square miles of rain forest are destroyed each day. At this rate of destruction, the losses in terms of all living things are staggering.

PUT ON YOUR THINKING CAP

PRIMARY   Look at the Animal Cards. Listen to your teacher read the information about each animal. Then listen to your teacher read the riddles. Decide which animal is being described in each riddle.

INTERMEDIATE   Write a riddle of your own about one of the animals found on the Animal Cards.

QUESTIONS WORTH RESEARCHING

PRIMARY   Kangaroos are marsupials. Research to find another animal that is a marsupial, and write two facts about it.

INTERMEDIATE   Tree kangaroos and koalas both live in Australia. List five ways in which these animals are alike. List five ways in which they are different.

ANIMAL CARD RIDDLES:

1. I still can't believe that I saw it,
   It's something I'll never forget,
   The face looked much like a fox's face,
   But it flew through the air like a jet!

2. Those eyes, those eyes, those big wide eyes,
   Just stared at me in wild surprise.
   The smallest monkey in the world
   Hung on the branches, fingers curled!

3. Although its fur is pretty, it would be a big mistake
   For hunters to continue to take and take and take.
   Its numbers are decreasing, and it really makes me sad,
   This cat of South America's 'bout the prettiest one we've had.

4. This very large animal looks a bit scary,
   But it's really quite gentle, though heavy and hairy.
   It can weigh as much as 400 pounds it is true,
   But its leaf-eating troop is a tree-nesting crew!

5. This animal has only two or three toes,
   It moves slowly from tree to tree as it goes;
   The algae that grows on its fur is quite green,
   Its one of the oddest things I've ever seen!

6. With a very long snout and a tail that is fat,
   This furry mammal looks much like a cat.
   It dines upon rodents, and reptiles, and birds,
   With its keen sight and smell too amazing for words!

7. The bones of its neck come right through its skin,
   They start to come out when they ought to be in.
   The thumb on each hand its other fingers face,
   And it moves through the night with slow lemur grace.

8. With heavy tails for balance high above the jungle floor,
   The need to move from tree to tree is far less of a chore.
   Jumping 20 feet across and up to 50 feet down
   Makes this a major athlete of any jungle town!

Answer Key, page 62

ANIMAL CARDS

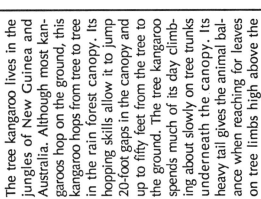

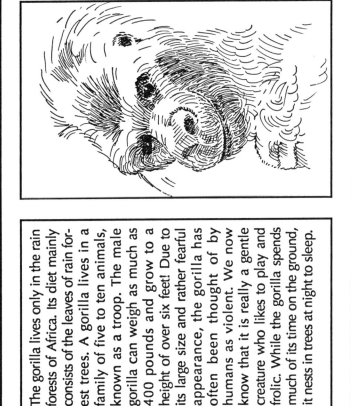

The gorilla lives only in the rain forests of Africa. Its diet mainly consists of the leaves of rain forest trees. A gorilla lives in a family of five to ten animals, known as a troop. The male gorilla can weigh as much as 400 pounds and grow to a height of over six feet! Due to its large size and rather fearful appearance, the gorilla has often been thought of by humans as violent. We now know that it is really a gentle creature who likes to play and frolic. While the gorilla spends much of its time on the ground, it nests in trees at night to sleep.

The tree kangaroo lives in the jungles of New Guinea and Australia. Although most kangaroos hop on the ground, this kangaroo hops from tree to tree in the rain forest canopy. Its hopping skills allow it to jump 20-foot gaps in the canopy and up to fifty feet from the tree to the ground. The tree kangaroo spends much of its day climbing about slowly on tree trunks underneath the canopy. Its heavy tail gives the animal balance when reaching for leaves on tree limbs high above the jungle floor.

The tarsier is the smallest monkey in the world. It lives in the rain forests of Asia and the Philippines. The tarsier is known for its unusually large eyes that look somewhat like those of an owl. The pads on its fingers and toes help it to hang on to branches and vines as it swings through the trees at night eating lizards and insects. Its name is derived from the fact that it has unusually long tarsal bones in its feet.

The two-toed and three-toed sloths live in the rain forests of Central and South America. The sloth is a very inactive animal and moves slowly. In fact, it is so slow that it can take an entire day for the animal simply to move from one tree to the next. The sloth often has a green tint to its fur from the algae that grows in it. Various insects, such as beetles and mites, also live in a sloth's fur.

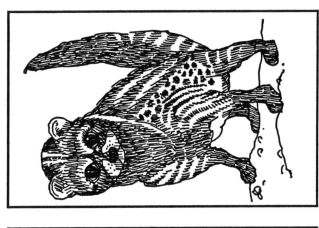

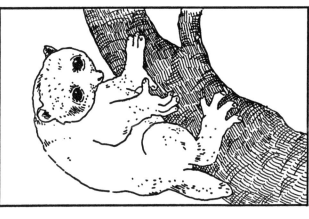

There are 850 different species in the bat family, of which the flying fox is a member. This mammal's head and body measure about a foot in length, while its wingspan can measure over five feet. Its face looks much like that of a fox. The flying fox is found in tropical rain forests throughout the world—with the exception of South America. It lives in groups that may number in the hundreds of thousands, eating mostly fruit, flower buds, nectar, and pollen. This animal is also known as the fruit bat.

This furry mammal of the rain forest looks much like a long, slender cat. Its tail is much fluffier, however, and its snout is more pointed. The color of the civet varies from black to brown to gray, with most species having dark spots or patches. The tail has rings of light and dark fur. The smallest civet is the African linsang and the largest is the binturong of Southeast Asia. This animal eats small reptiles, rodents, birds, frogs, and insects. The civet can hear and see extremely well and is an excellent hunter.

The ocelot is a member of the cat family. It lives primarily in the forests of South America, but can also be found in parts of southern Arizona and southern Texas in the United States. The ocelot can grow to over a foot tall at the shoulder and about three and one-half feet long. Its diet consists of mice, rats, rabbits, deer, monkeys, and snakes. The tropical ocelot also eats agoutis. Fur trappers have greatly decreased the ocelot's numbers.

The potto is the smallest animal living in the rain forests of western Africa. It is a member of the group of animals called slow lemurs, but looks more like a sloth than a monkey. Its most unusual feature is the tips of the spinal bones in its neck which project through the skin. It is able to grip branches tightly as its thumb faces its other fingers. The potto usually lives in pairs and is most active at night. Its diet consists of fruits, eggs, and a variety of insects.

BIRDS

BACKGROUND

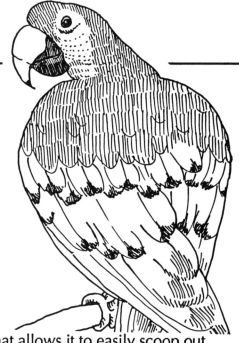

Many colorful and exotic birds live in the understory of the tropical rain forest. Although there are many more species of birds in the rain forest than in any other type of forest, they are often difficult for humans to see. This is because they live and feed in the dense foliage high above the forest floor. Many rain forest birds spend their summers in Europe or North America and their winters at home in the rain forest.

The parrot is probably the best-known bird of the rain forest. Its heavy, hooked beak is an adaptation that allows it to easily scoop out fruit from a peel and crack seeds. More than 300 species of parrot are found in the rain forest in a wide variety of bright colors. Because the parrot is able to mimic human speech, it has become a popular domestic pet. Some species of parrot, however, have become endangered due to over-collecting and habitat destruction. For each parrot successfully captured and transported to a pet shop, many others had to die along the way.

PUT ON YOUR THINKING CAP

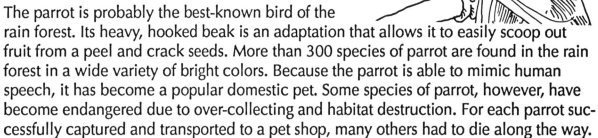

PRIMARY/INTERMEDIATE REMEMBER THAT?

Look carefully at the Rain Forest drawing (page 13) for one minute, then put the drawing away and answer these questions.

1. How many parrots are in the picture?
2. Is the toucan on the right or left side of the page?
3. How many flying birds did you see?
4. What is the total number of birds in the picture?
5. How many different types of flowers did you see?
6. How many birds are feeding on flowers?
7. How many trees did you count?
8. What other kinds of living things did you see?
9. How many insects could you find?
10. Which animals are eating fruit?

QUESTIONS WORTH RESEARCHING

PRIMARY The hoatzin is an odd-looking character. Draw a picture of a hoatzin and tell one interesting fact about it.

INTERMEDIATE Compare the toucan to the parrot. Explain their likenesses and differences.

RAIN FOREST

C CANOPY

BACKGROUND

The cover formed by the tree tops of the rain forest is called the canopy. This layer of treetops stands between 100 and 200 feet off the ground and is home to two-thirds of the plants and animals living in the rain forest. The thickness of the foliage at this level prevents sunlight from reaching the lower levels of the forest. The main job of the canopy is to capture sunlight and change it into food for the trees through a process called photosynthesis. When sunlight does penetrate the canopy and reach the forest floor, small trees and plants grow into a tangled mass called a jungle.

Many of the creatures that live in the rain forest spend their entire life in the canopy—they might never move to the forest ground. Entire food chains begin, develop, and die in this layer. In fact, scientists speculate that a large percentage of all of the plants and animals found on Earth live in the rain forest canopy.

PUT ON YOUR THINKING CAP

PRIMARY   1. The word canopy has several different meanings. Draw a picture of something that you think of when you hear the word canopy.

2. Many words in the English language have more than one meaning. With a partner, work to find the different meanings for each of the following words. Match these words with their meanings by lining up the fruit (page 15) beneath the trees below.

1. watch   2. back   3. take   4. mark   5. kid   6. crown

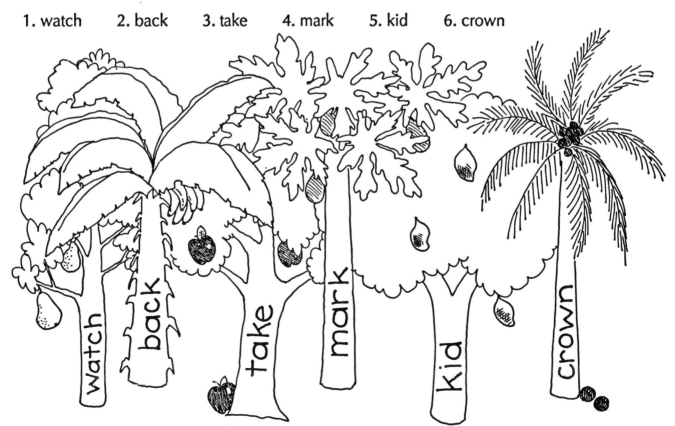

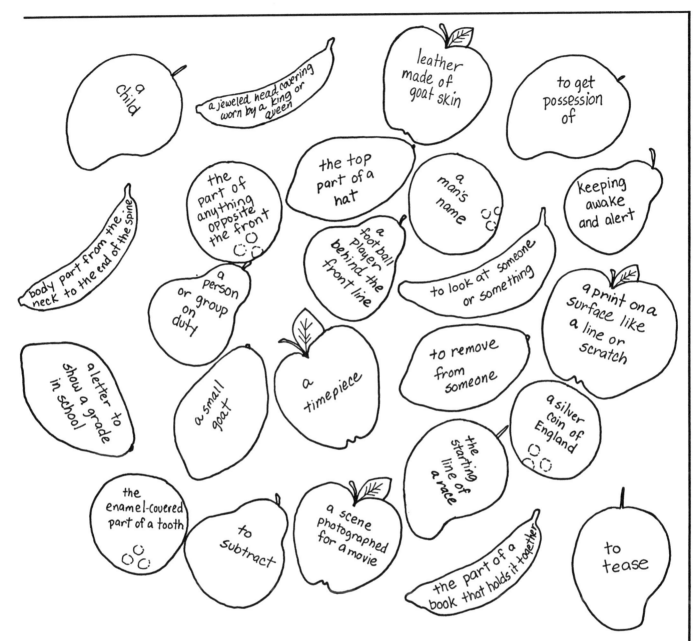

INTERMEDIATE Many words that are related to the study of the rain forest have multiple meanings. Create two sentences using each of the following words. Each sentence should express a completely different meaning.

1. material   2. root   3. clear(ed)   4. destroyer   5. plot

QUESTIONS WORTH RESEARCHING

PRIMARY Name two types of trees that can grow to over 100 feet tall and are found in the rain forest. Give two facts about each tree.

INTERMEDIATE Find out more about photosynthesis. Create a diagram to help explain the process to someone else.

DEFORESTATION

BACKGROUND

Rain forests are important to humans for a variety of reasons. The plants that grow in the rain forest provide ingredients for prescription drugs and give us spices, food, wood, oils, and fibers. Rain forests are home to a majority of the plant and animal species of the world. These forests also help to control worldwide climate and water cycles. Why, then, are they being cut down at a rate of over fifty acres per minute? This process of clearing forest trees by cutting and burning is called deforestation and is occurring for several reasons.

Commercial loggers are clearing the forest in order to sell its beautiful exotic woods, such as mahogany and teak, to other countries. These trees grow sporadically throughout the rain forest and are extremely difficult to cut down without also destroying many of the surrounding trees. It is estimated that twelve million acres of rain forest are logged for commercial purposes each year.

Farming claims another 20 million acres of rain forest per year. Poor, landless farmers follow the roads created by loggers and clear forest land on which to farm. These farms are small and produce just enough food for the farmer's own family. Once the rain forest vegetation is cleared from these lands, however, the needed nutrients and minerals in the soil are easily washed away by torrential tropical rains. Within three to four years, the soil becomes worthless, and the farmers move on to clear a new patch of land.

New roads and cattle ranching also account for large portions of rain forests being cleared each year.

PUT ON YOUR THINKING CAP

PRIMARY/INTERMEDIATE Write two tongue twisters about the rain forest. Practice with this one.

"Farming families furrow former forests, forming farm fields."

QUESTIONS WORTH RESEARCHING

PRIMARY Find out if the land you live on today was once covered by trees. If so, what kind of trees were they?

INTERMEDIATE Do some research to complete the chart.

Type Of Tree	Where It Is Found	Uses	Years To Maturity
1. Pine	_____	_____	_____
	_____	_____	
2. Mahogany	_____	_____	_____
	_____	_____	
3. Teak	_____	_____	_____
	_____	_____	
4. Sequoia	_____	_____	_____
	_____	_____	
5. Ash	_____	_____	_____
	_____	_____	
6. Rosewood	_____	_____	_____
	_____	_____	
7. Oak	_____	_____	_____
	_____	_____	
8. Eucalyptus	_____	_____	_____
	_____	_____	

Evaluate: Rank the trees in order, beginning with those we should be able to harvest freely and continuing with those we should seldom or never harvest. Be prepared to defend your selections in a class discussion.

EMERGENTS

BACKGROUND

The tops of the tallest trees in the rain forest form the highest layer of the canopy. These trees are called emergents, and this forest layer is called the emergent layer.

Emergents are giant trees which typically grow to a height of 115 feet—although some may grow to over 200 feet! They stand high above the majority of other rain forest plants and are exposed to strong winds and high, constantly changing temperatures. There are usually only one or two of these enormous trees in each acre of forest. As their root systems are often quite shallow, stormy conditions may cause emergents to uproot easily.

Ferns, mosses, orchids, and other plants grow on the emergent's tall, straight trunk. Vines also grow along the forest floor and intertwine from tree to tree, eventually tying groups of trees together. If one tree from the entwined group is cut down, it may pull other trees down with it.

PUT ON YOUR THINKING CAP

PRIMARY   Let's go on a Fact Safari! It is important to carefully look at all the facts before guessing the answer to a question. Using the background information on emergents as your source, which questions can you answer without guessing? Write "yes" next to the questions you can answer. Write "no" next to those questions whose answers you must guess.

1._____ What do scientists call the top layer of the rain forest?

2._____ What are stilt roots?

3._____ How many emergent trees are usually found in an acre of rain forest?

4._____ What kinds of plants can be found growing on emergents?

5._____ Why are tall trees of the rain forest called emergents?

INTERMEDIATE   Imagine that you have just arrived at the edge of the rain forest. You are going to walk through a small section of the rain forest with a friend. Name, draw, and label the things you see as you enter. List the sounds and smells you remember.

QUESTIONS WORTH RESEARCHING

PRIMARY   The Amazon Forest is the largest remaining rain forest in the world. Do some research and write two facts about it.

INTERMEDIATE   Compare an orchid to a daisy. List and discuss their differences and similarities. Sketch a picture of each one.

19

BACKGROUND

The world's rain forests contain a greater variety of plants than any other place on Earth. Many of the foods we eat today, in fact, are native to the rain forest: tea, coffee, oranges, pineapples, grapefruits, rice, corn, and sugarcane all originated in rain forests. The smallest rain forest tree, the cacao, provides us with chocolate. All of these products are now grown commercially throughout the world. If you were to visit outdoor markets in places such as Peru or Thailand, however, you would see many different types of rain forest fruits still unknown in the United States.

Fruit is not the only rain forest product enjoyed worldwide. Spices such as cinnamon, cardamom, paprika, and black pepper all originated in the rain forest.

PUT ON YOUR THINKING CAP

PRIMARY   Brainstorm and come up with a list of your favorite fruits. Research to find out to what areas of the world your favorite fruits are native. You may choose to brainstorm a list of favorite vegetables instead.

INTERMEDIATE   Tell whether each of the following foods grows above or below the ground: apple, avocado, banana, broccoli, cardamom, carrot, date, fig, guava, grapefruit, horseradish, lemon, macadamia nut, mango, onion, passion fruit, peanut, parsnip, rice, sweet potato, sugar beet, tangerine, tomato, yam.

QUESTIONS WORTH RESEARCHING

PRIMARY/INTERMEDIATE   Complete the chart advertising a nutritious rain forest food of your choice. The food could be grown and sold to help poor farmers feed their families without endangering the rain forest in any way.

Description of food

Ways to prepare food

Where to find food

Why eat it?

Picture

Ad to sell food

GREENHOUSE EFFECT

BACKGROUND

When we think of greenhouses, we think of large glass structures used for growing plants. It is, indeed, from these structures that the "greenhouse effect" gets its name. The glass walls and roof of a greenhouse trap the warmth of the sun, creating a warm, moist climate for the plants inside. Although the glass allows the rays of the sun inside, it doesn't allow much of the heat produced by those rays to leave the greenhouse.

Our Earth is warmed by the sun in much the same way, although our atmosphere allows the excess heat of the sun's rays to return to space. In the past few years, however, scientists have determined that more of this heat is being trapped in the Earth's atmosphere. This trapping of heat is known as the greenhouse effect.

As a result of the greenhouse effect, scientists predict that three things may happen. The Earth's temperatures may rise. The weather may actually change in parts of the world. (For example, there may not be enough rain to grow corn in Iowa.) The water level of the world's oceans might rise—maybe as much as one to four feet—during the next ten years.

The greenhouse effect is occurring because of changes in our Earth's atmosphere. The blanket of air around the Earth is called the atmosphere. It is made up of about 78% nitrogen and 20% oxygen and protects the Earth from the sun's harmful rays. The atmosphere also contains a a small amount of carbon dioxide. Plants use carbon dioxide to make food.

The Earth has always had just enough carbon dioxide to retain the delicate natural balance between the amount of carbon dioxide on the Earth and in the atmosphere. People, however, have introduced increasingly large amounts of carbon dioxide into the atmosphere—upsetting nature's plan. When people burn fossil fuels such as coal, oil, and natural gas to run factories, power plants, cars, and homes, excess carbon dioxide rises into the atmosphere. With this recent buildup of carbon dioxide, less heat can escape the Earth and the planet begins to resemble a giant greenhouse.

PUT ON YOUR THINKING CAP

PRIMARY   CREATE YOUR OWN GREENHOUSE
You will need:
1. an aquarium
2. a piece of plastic larger than the aquarium
3. thermometer
4. tape

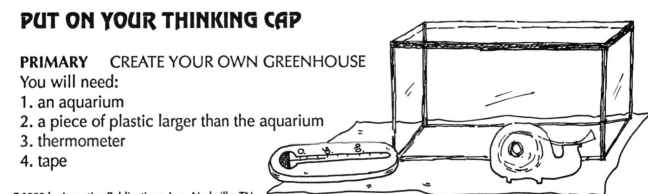

Follow these steps:
1. Punch several holes into the plastic sheet.
2. Place the thermometer inside the aquarium. Read and record the temperature.
3. Cover the aquarium with the plastic sheet and tape around the edges to seal.
4. Place the aquarium in the sun. After several hours, record the temperature again.

How do your first and second temperature readings compare?

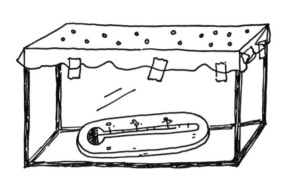 

INTERMEDIATE   Scientists fear that the greenhouse effect will cause oceans to rise as hotter air begins to melt glaciers in areas such as Greenland. To find out more about this problem, conduct the following experiment.

THE GREAT GLACIER MELT

You will need:
1. four to six ice cubes   2. one small glass   3. cold water

Follow these steps:
1. Place four ice cubes into a small empty glass.
2. Fill with cold water.
3. Place the full glass of water on a clean, dry table, and check it every 15 minutes.
4. Describe your findings.

What do you think will happen to the oceans if the glaciers begin to melt?

Why would this be a problem?

QUESTIONS WORTH RESEARCHING

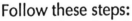

PRIMARY   Find out how plants use carbon dioxide. Describe the process.

INTERMEDIATE   How does the burning of forests contribute to the greenhouse effect?

HUNTER-GATHERERS

BACKGROUND

While most of the world's societies rely on agriculture to produce their food supplies, there are still small groups of people who live by hunting animals, fishing, and gathering wild plants. These people are known as hunter-gatherers. Many of these groups live in the rain forest. When they have eaten most of the food to be found in a particular area, they simply move to another part of the forest. As they move from place to place, they build temporary huts of sticks and leaves.

Hunter-gatherers usually live in groups of about thirty. Although they may briefly visit larger, permanent villages near the edges of the rain forest to conduct trade, they don't like the heat of these villages and are distrustful of the water. The drinking water of the villages may make these hunter-gatherers ill; however, when they return to the forest, they usually become well again. As more rain forest areas are logged and developed, hunter-gatherer territories are being destroyed.

PUT ON YOUR THINKING CAP

PRIMARY   The following words remind us of hunter-gatherers. Think of a rhyming word to go along with each one, and then write a poem about the life of the hunter-gatherers using some of your rhyming word pairs.

1. HUNT   _____

2. FOOD   _____

3. NUT   _____

4. BERRY   _____

5. ROAM   _____

6. HUT   _____

7. RAIN   _____

8. STICK   _____

INTERMEDIATE   If you could not buy any of your food commercially but had to grow or gather it yourself, in what part of the United States would you want to live? List the foods from that area that you could eat if you had to hunt for them or gather them.

How would you make each of the following foods a part of your diet?
1. Milk   2. Meat   3. Fruits   4. Vegetables   5. Breads and Cereals

QUESTIONS WORTH RESEARCHING

PRIMARY   What does the term "hunter-gatherer" mean? Who are the hunter-gatherers? Tell something about them.

INTERMEDIATE   Name two or three African hunter-gatherer tribes. Tell something interesting about each group.

They use leaves to shingle their huts.

They gather and eat the fruit from the rain forests

They make nets from vines to trap prey.

ITHOMIINE

BACKGROUND

The brightly colored ithomiine (ih-tho-mee-ine) butterfly lives in tropical rain forests. Its bold patterns and bright colors act as a warning to would-be predators. This butterfly not only tastes bad, it contains dangerous chemicals, as well. When a predator eats this bad-tasting or poisonous butterfly, it learns to avoid preying upon all butterflies that look like the ithomiine, thus giving the ithomiine a better chance to survive.

Mimic, or look-alike, ithomiine butterflies live alongside the genuine ithomiine butterflies in the rain forest. These butterflies look almost like the originals, but are not poisonous and don't taste bad. How does this help the ithomiine look-alikes?

PUT ON YOUR THINKING CAP

PRIMARY   Create your own original butterfly below. Invent two facts about the butterfly you have created.

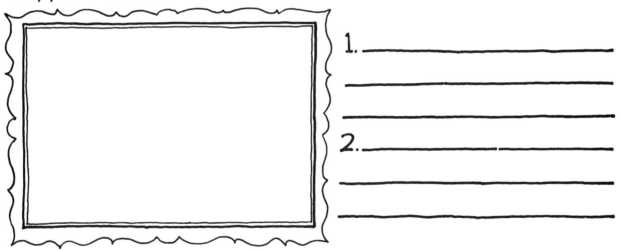

1. _____

_____

_____

2. _____

_____

_____

INTERMEDIATE   An idiom is a saying that has an intended meaning quite unlike its literal one. Draw a picture of both the intended and literal meanings of the following idiom:

"I have butterflies in my stomach."

QUESTIONS WORTH RESEARCHING

PRIMARY   Do some research, and draw pictures of two types of butterflies other than the ithomiine that live in the rain forest. Label them.

1._____   2._____

INTERMEDIATE   In one square mile of rain forest in Peru, scientists have estimated that more than 1,500 species of butterflies may be found. Do some research to find out about the types of butterflies that can be found in your state. Name one and give several facts about it. Illustrate your findings.

J JUST A DREAM

BACKGROUND

Just A Dream (Boston: Houghton Mifflin Co., 1990) is a book written and illustrated by Chris Van Allsburg, the author of such children's favorites as *Polar Express* and *Jumanji*. While *Just A Dream* does not directly deal with the topic of tropical rain forests, it does address the interconnected nature of all aspects of our environment. It focuses on the importance of ecologically sound practices that children can follow, such as planting trees. Read *Just a Dream* as a springboard to the activities that follow.

PUT ON YOUR THINKING CAP

PRIMARY   Brainstorm a list of activities that you can do to help save the forests of the world.

INTERMEDIATE   In *Just A Dream*, Walter dreams of a future with tiny airplanes, robots to do chores, and machines to make jelly doughnuts. Draw a picture of the future that you would like to see in 100 years.

QUESTIONS WORTH RESEARCHING

PRIMARY   Draw pictures of a rain forest today and how you think a rain forest will look in fifty years if humans continue to destroy it.

Present

Future

INTERMEDIATE   Research to find out how the loss of the rain forest affects the ecology of the entire world.

THE GREAT KAPOK TREE

BACKGROUND

The story of *The Great Kapok Tree* explains the effects of deforestation in an easy-to-understand format. The author, Lynne Cherry, traveled to the Amazon rain forest to research her illustrations and has done an amazing job of bringing the plight of the rain forest one step closer to home. Begin this exercise by reading *The Great Kapok Tree* (New York: Harcourt, Brace, Jovanovich Publishers, 1990).

PUT ON YOUR THINKING CAP

PRIMARY   Put a circle around things you would find in a rain forest. Put an X over anything else.

polar   bear

coatimundi

sloth

worm

robin

jaguar

toucan

horse

tree frog

parrot

INTERMEDIATE   SIZE WISE

Compare each of the following rain forest dwellers to the size of your foot. Decide if it is larger or smaller. Make a check in the correct column.

	Larger	Smaller
1. POISON ARROW FROG		
2. HOATZIN		
3. PUFFBIRD		
4. BLUE MORPHO BUTTERFLY		
5. RAFFLESIA PLANT		
6. ROSY PERIWINKLES		
7. QUETZAL		
8. OKAPI		
9. UALANG		
10. PLANTAIN		
11. PASSION FRUIT		
12. TOUCAN		
13. PAPAYA		
14. MACAW		
15. LEAF-TAILED GECKO		

QUESTIONS WORTH RESEARCHING

PRIMARY   Choose an animal mentioned in *The Great Kapok Tree* and draw it. On the back of your picture, write two facts about your animal.

INTERMEDIATE   Find out about the work of Chico Mendes. Write a newspaper article about his life.

L LOCATIONS

BACKGROUND

The world's rain forests are in danger of disappearing. Although they now cover only six percent of the Earth's land, over half of the species of plants and animals on the planet live in these forests. At one time, rain forests covered land twice the size of the United States—about four billion acres spread across equatorial regions in Mexico, Central America, South America, Africa, Malaysia, the Philippines, southeastern Asia, Australia, and Papua New Guinea. Half of this land had been destroyed by 1990, and another 51 million forested acres of rain forest are lost each year.

Today, the South American rain forest accounts for about half of all remaining rain forest lands. Most other forested regions have been divided into small pieces. The South American rain forest is the largest uninterrupted tract of wilderness in the world. It is located primarily in the Amazon basin and spans the countries of Brazil, Peru, Bolivia, Colombia, Ecuador, Venezuela, and Guyana.

Twenty percent of the remaining rain forest can be found on the continent of Africa—primarily in the country of Zaire. Southeastern Asia houses another twenty-five percent of rain forest, with that continent's largest portion in the country of Indonesia.

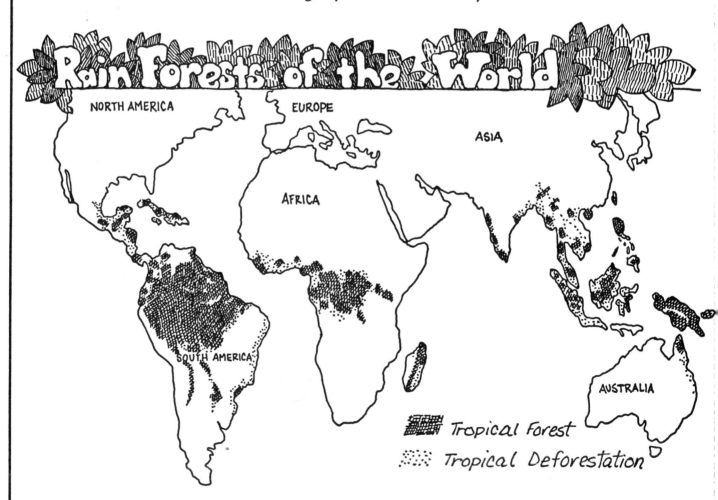

Rain Forests of the World

NORTH AMERICA   EUROPE   ASIA

AFRICA

SOUTH AMERICA

AUSTRALIA

▦ Tropical Forest
░ Tropical Deforestation

PUT ON YOUR THINKING CAP

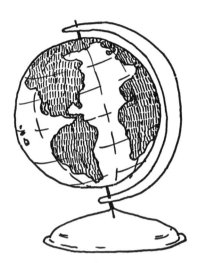

PRIMARY   Using a globe, point out and name the countries where rain forests can be found today.

INTERMEDIATE   Brainstorm a list of information that you already know about rain forests. After this list is complete, partner with two other people to research this list for accuracy. Good sources to use include:

1. *The Rain Forest* by Billy Goodman (New York: Tern Enterprises, 1991).

2. *Our Endangered Planet—Tropical Rain Forests* by Cornelia F. Mutel and Mary M. Rodgers (Minneapolis, MN: Lerner Publications, 1991).

3. *Exploring Our World—Tropical Forests* by Terry Jennings and Marshall Cavendish (New York: Freeport, 1986).

Write each statement you come up with on a small piece of paper. Research the statement to assess its truth. If the statement is true, write the title of the book and the page number that will provide you with evidence of its validity.

If the statement is false, write down a corrected statement and the title of the book and page number that will support your new claims.

QUESTIONS WORTH RESEARCHING

PRIMARY   In what regions of the United States do forests grow? How are these forests different from tropical rain forests?

INTERMEDIATE   Are any rain forests located in the United States? Why or why not?

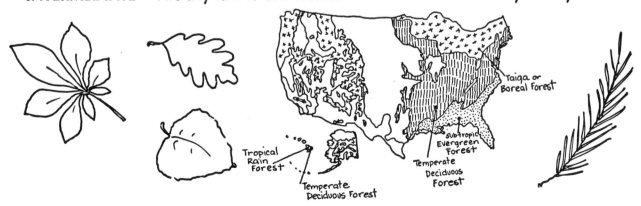

MEDICINE

BACKGROUND

Although you may not realize it, people all over the world use rain forest products almost every day. Some of the most important materials to come from rain forests are plants used to make medicines. Many of the drugs that we use today to treat such diseases as high blood pressure and leukemia were originally made from rain forest products. Scientists are hopeful that someday they will find a cure for cancer among the plants of these forests. There are still hundreds of thousands of tropical plants that are yet to be examined for possible medical benefits.

One rain forest plant in particular has been of great value to children with a cancerous blood disease called lymphocytic leukemia. The leaves of the rosy periwinkle are used to make a successful anti-leukemia drug. Without this drug, many children with leukemia would die, but with the new drug, there is a 99 percent chance that the cancer will go into remission. About fifteen tons of periwinkle leaves are needed to make one ounce of the drug. It would have been an enormous loss to our world if the destruction of the rain forest had prevented scientists from ever discovering the medical value of the periwinkle.

PUT ON YOUR THINKING CAP

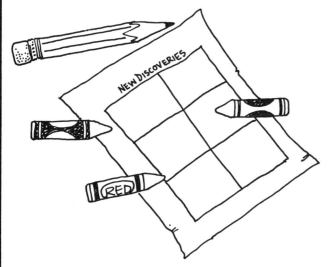

PRIMARY/INTERMEDIATE Scientists have still not seen many of the plants and animals that exist in the rain forest. Using the New Discoveries activity sheet (page 35), pretend that each of the made-up words is a recently discovered rain forest plant or animal. Draw and color each one in as great detail as you possibly can in the space provided.

As a bonus, write an interesting characteristic about each "new" plant or animal on the back of each picture.

QUESTIONS WORTH RESEARCHING

PRIMARY/INTERMEDIATE Draw a periwinkle. On a map, find the area of the world where the periwinkle grows.

NEW DISCOVERIES

OLOPKO	BILGOP
PODKIN	LIGDODE
EFDEEN	CODFUR

NATURE-BASED TOURISM

BACKGROUND

In many poor, underdeveloped countries, rain forests are being cut down in order to help the people survive. Small tribes of poor farmers slash and burn patches of forest in order to have land on which to plant crops to feed their families. Local loggers sell exotic trees to earn a better living for themselves and their families. For many, deforestation is seen as necessary for survival.

In the past few years, however, a new rain forest-based industry has developed: nature-based tourism is becoming a way for rain forest countries to earn money while protecting the forest and all that lives there. Tourists from countries that do not have rain forests pay to visit rain forest preserves. These preserves are carefully managed and protected. Government officials are now beginning to realize that preserving the rain forest may bring in money needed for economic development. This rain forest conservation will greatly enhance the health of our entire planet.

PUT ON YOUR THINKING CAP

PRIMARY Recycle aluminum cans or newspapers to raise enough money (usually $30-$50) to adopt an acre of rain forest. Write to The Nature Conservancy to find out more about this program. Their address is 1815 North Lynn Street, Arlington, Virginia 22209.

INTERMEDIATE You and a team of two friends have been chosen to design an advertising brochure for travel agencies around the world. You are to advertise "A Rain Forest Adventure." Your brochure should highlight what sights travelers can expect to see on their rain forest tour. Other information should include cost, accommodations, sights on the way, meals, etc. Make the brochure eye-catching!

QUESTIONS WORTH RESEARCHING

PRIMARY/INTERMEDIATE By saving one acre of rain forest, how many species of plants and animals might be saved? How many would be saved in ten acres of rain forest?

ORGANIZATIONS

BACKGROUND

There are many ways that we can all help the rain forest to survive. We can show support for products that provide the people of the rain forest with a profit without harming the forests in any way. We can stop buying products that are destroying the rain forest. We can write letters to companies whose policies we disapprove of and to political figures who can influence rain forest destruction.

Of course, we all know that we must REDUCE, REUSE, and RECYCLE in order to preserve our planet. People in the United States throw out 432,000 tons of garbage every day! By recycling our garbage, we can save energy and help conserve our world's natural resources.

Another important step we can take is to plant trees. Trees help to use some of the excess carbon dioxide made by the burning of coal, natural gas, oil, and rain forest trees. This will, in turn, halt the effects of global warming.

Remember, you are not alone. Concerned citizens all over the world have banded together to form organizations that protect our world's resources. They include:

Conservation International
1015 18th St. NW, Suite 1000
Washington, D.C. 20036

Cultural Survival, Inc.
53A Church Street
Cambridge, Massachusetts 02138

Environmental Defense Fund
257 Park Avenue South
New York, New York 10010

Rainforest Action Network
301 Broadway, Suite A
San Francisco, California 94133

The Nature Conservancy
1815 North Lynn Street
Arlington, Virginia 22209

Rainforest Alliance
270 Lafayette Street, Suite 512
New York, New York 10012

PUT ON YOUR THINKING CAP

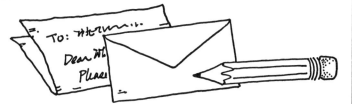

PRIMARY/INTERMEDIATE

1. Write to one of the organizations listed on page 38 to receive information on how you can help our planet live a long and healthy life.

2. Complete the Word Find. Circle the 12 hidden words associated with the rain forest:

1. canopy	5. equator	9. habitats
2. understory	6. emergent	10. sloth
3. toucan	7. deforestation	11. rafflesia
4. Amazon	8. periwinkle	12. tree frog

Z	Q	D	G	A	H	Q	L	R	A	K	P	S	U	N	K	E	V	R
G	T	A	D	E	M	E	R	G	E	N	T	H	I	B	R	H	I	G
O	U	V	S	Q	T	A	M	R	A	F	F	L	E	S	I	A	F	V
R	G	K	M	U	G	P	Z	D	B	H	K	O	P	N	S	B	E	A
F	T	S	F	A	N	U	N	O	J	P	E	R	T	L	U	I	H	N
E	W	B	G	T	Q	M	C	A	N	O	P	Y	W	N	Y	T	C	X
E	L	E	Z	O	U	T	D	Y	C	G	D	F	A	C	O	A	F	I
R	Y	P	E	R	I	W	I	N	K	L	E	C	X	L	O	T	K	Z
T	I	H	O	P	E	U	S	J	M	Q	U	V	S	B	D	S	P	J
G	C	L	M	J	C	K	O	L	D	O	M	B	E	X	H	K	N	R
W	J	A	O	D	U	Y	R	O	T	S	R	E	D	N	U	E	J	G
G	D	E	F	O	R	E	S	T	A	T	I	O	N	A	Z	H	U	S
Z	B	G	C	T	I	R	U	B	P	M	V	U	E	L	W	B	C	Q

Answer Key, page 62

QUESTION WORTH RESEARCHING

PRIMARY/INTERMEDIATE   Do some research to find out what types of products are produced at the expense of the rain forests. List them.

PEOPLE

BACKGROUND

Many of the people indigenous to the rain forests live today in much the same way as their ancestors have lived for centuries. As modern civilization expands into regions of the rain forest formerly untouched by the outside world, however, many of these tribes begin to lose touch with their traditional ways. Some young people even leave their rain forest tribes to live in villages or large cities.

The largest tribe of the African forest people is the Baka. The Baka live primarily within the forest itself, foraging food and shelter from the land. They do spend part of the year in permanent villages near the edge of the forest, exchanging meat for such items as tools and utensils as it is forbidden by the tribe for the Baka people to eat meat they have killed themselves. The Baka are also honey gatherers and frequently climb trees over 100 feet tall to smoke out bees with burning leaves to gather their honey. This can be a dangerous job! As the Baka are not forbidden to eat this self-gathered food, much of the honey is eaten before it is even brought back to the tribe.

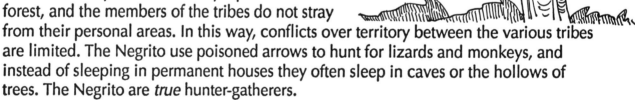

In the dense and mountainous tropical forest regions of Malaysia in southeastern Asia live the Negrito. These people live in tribes of approximately sixty people who roam the forest in search of food. They do not move about the forest freely, however. Each tribe in the region has its own territory of about twenty square miles of forest, and the members of the tribes do not stray from their personal areas. In this way, conflicts over territory between the various tribes are limited. The Negrito use poisoned arrows to hunt for lizards and monkeys, and instead of sleeping in permanent houses they often sleep in caves or the hollows of trees. The Negrito are *true* hunter-gatherers.

The Senoi people of Malaysia live quite differently from their Negrito neighbors. Instead of hunting and gathering their food, these people are involved in shifting cultivation. They cut down and burn a small patch of forest, using the ash to fertilize the ground. Eventually, regional heavy rains wash much of the nutrients from the soil. After planting crops in one area for two or three years, the Senoi are forced to move on—to burn yet another patch of forest and farm once again. When the forest has been completely destroyed, these people will need to develop a new way of life.

Of course, these are only a few of the wide variety of people practicing different types of low-level agriculture or hunting and gathering who live in rain forests around the world.

PUT ON YOUR THINKING CAP

PRIMARY   A JUNGLE OF LETTERS
The letters below are really sentences crowded together like the plant life of the jungle.
Circle the words to discover messages about forest people.

1. Forestpeoplemayeathoney.

2. Theyclimbtalltrees.

3. Somepeoplemaybesmall.

4. Theylivewhereitishot.

5. Somemayliveincavesortrees.

6. Theforestiswarmandpretty.

7. Somepeoplemaycatchfishtoeat.

8. Manyanimalsandplantsliveintheforest.

9. Somepeopleoftheforestmayfarm.

10. Peoplewalkintheforestlookingforfood.

INTERMEDIATE   TRIBAL MESSAGES
Cross out the names of rain forest tribes in the puzzle below. Circle the left-over words
and write the secret message.

_____

_____

T	H	E	E	F	E	F	O	R	E	S	T	S
P	E	O	P	L	E	S	K	A	Y	A	P	O
B	A	K	A	L	I	V	E	S	E	N	O	I
I	N	N	E	G	R	I	T	O	W	A	R	M
B	A	M	B	U	T	I	J	U	N	G	L	E
A	R	E	A	S	M	B	U	T	I	A	N	D
U	N	D	E	R	W	A	U	R	A	T	H	E
F	O	R	E	S	T	S	C	A	N	O	P	Y

Answer Key, page 63

QUESTIONS WORTH RESEARCHING

PRIMARY/INTERMEDIATE   Find out about the lives of the Kayapo. Where do they
live? In what ways are their lives different from ours?

QUESTION: "WHY SAVE THE RAIN FOREST?"

BACKGROUND

There are many good reasons for saving the world's rain forests from destruction. One of the most pressing reasons is that the rain forest is an important factor in the Earth's delicate natural balance. Millions of people around the world are unaware of the rain forest's importance to the planet and continue to destroy this natural wonder for profit.

Think about the following reasons for preserving rain forests:

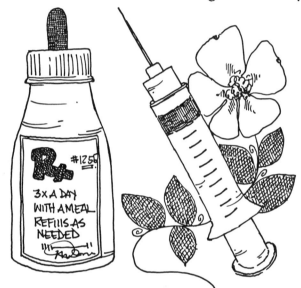

1. Rain forest loss may greatly change weather patterns throughout the world.
2. The culture and traditions of the forest people will be lost with the disappearance of these forests.
3. Many important products, such as valuable medicines, come from the rain forest's plants.
4. Many animals depend on rain forests for their survival. When forests are destroyed, habitats are lost, thus endangering the lives of many animal species.
5. Loss of forests creates problems for nearby regions, the most serious of which are soil erosion and water pollution.

There are many other answers to the question, "Why save the rain forest?" These are just a few of them.

PUT ON YOUR THINKING CAP

PRIMARY   Create a poster advertising one important reason for saving the rain forest. It may be one of the reasons given here, or another reason you have discovered.

SAVE THE RAIN FOREST

INTERMEDIATE   Complete the Alphabet Mystery game.

ALPHABET MYSTERY

Follow the directions provided to answer this question: "What type of animal travels from North America to the South American rain forest each year?"

X A B F M L R G X

1. Change all the original X's to S's.

2. Change all the original F's to G's.

3. Change all the original B's to N's.

4. Change all the original A's to O's.

5. Change all the original M's to B's.

6. Change all the original G's to D's.

7. Change all the original L's to I's.

Answer Key, page 63

QUESTIONS WORTH RESEARCHING

PRIMARY   Draw a picture of a rain forest animal that is considered an endangered species due to habitat loss.

INTERMEDIATE   Do some research to find two reasons, other than the ones previously mentioned, for saving the rain forest.

RUBBER TREES

BACKGROUND

Rubber trees are native to the Amazon. The natural material for rubber, known as latex, is extracted from these trees. Latex is a milky-white sap that flows just beneath the bark of the rubber tree. Latex serves as the tree's natural pesticide and is released when the tree is cut to keep insects away. Although poisonous to insects, humans found a way to make rubber from the latex during the nineteenth century. When rubber was first produced, it was not a huge commercial success. It became brittle and broke when exposed to the cold. When the weather was hot, the rubber became gooey. It wasn't until the process of vulcanization was developed that rubber became a durable and flexible commercial product.

During the late 1800s, rubber tree seeds were taken to Southeast Asia, ending the Amazon rubber boom. Although only one percent of Brazil's rubber is produced locally today, many rubber tappers still live in the Amazon rain forest. Each tapper is paid to extract rubber from a tract of land about 750 acres in size. These tappers do not want to see the rain forest destroyed and may sometimes have confrontations with local cattle ranchers who try to clear land for livestock grazing.

PUT ON YOUR THINKING CAP

PRIMARY   Brainstorm a list of products used in America that are made from rubber. Alphabetize your list.

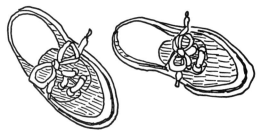

INTERMEDIATE   Complete the Anagram activity (page 45) in groups of two or three students.

QUESTIONS WORTH RESEARCHING

PRIMARY   From where does the United States buy most of its rubber?

INTERMEDIATE   Do some research to find out how the process of vulcanization works.

ANAGRAMS

An anagram is a word created by rearranging the letters of a different word or phrase. Using the letters in the phrase RUBBER TREES' LATEX, create anagrams which answer the following questions. For each answer, you may use each letter only the number of times it appears in the original phrase. (For example, there are only two B's in the phrase "Rubber Trees' Latex." Your response, therefore, should only use the letter B twice.)

1. Collected by the IRS _____

2. Person up to bat_____

3. Begin_____

4. A bully (slang) _____

5. Confidence_____

6. Public road_____

7. To speak a sound _____

8. To take something not belonging to you_____

9. Second largest state in the U.S.A. _____

10. Spoiled child _____

* Answer Key, page 63

SLASH-AND-BURN FARMING

BACKGROUND

In some cases, a few rich land barons own much of the productive farmland in the tropics. They typically hire poor farmhands to work their plantations and large cattle ranches. The rest of the land has such poor soil that it is nearly impossible to use it for growing good crops. The independent farmer must look elsewhere for land on which to farm and often turns to the rain forest as a source of land for planting crops.

In the rain forests, many farmers practice slash-and-burn farming. When practicing this method of farming, the farmer claims a small patch of land, cuts down the trees, and burns the existing vegetation to create ash. The ash is then used to fertilize the soil. This soil only remains fertile for a couple of years. Once the crops have stripped the soil of its nutrients, the farmer must move on to slash-and-burn another claim. This is one of the most common ways that rain forests are destroyed today.

PUT ON YOUR THINKING CAP

PRIMARY   Slash-and-burn farmers need to be able to start the vegetation on fire once it has been cut down. Pretend your family has a pet fire-breathing dragon. Draw it here. Name it and list three ways that it could be useful to your family.

INTERMEDIATE   Fire is a powerful force. List the positive and negative aspects of fire. If you had the power to determine if fire would remain on Earth or disappear forever, what would you choose? Why?

QUESTIONS WORTH RESEARCHING

PRIMARY/INTERMEDIATE   What is a plantation? Where can we find plantations in the United States? How did pioneers clear land in colonial America? How was this technique different from the slash-and-burn farming of today?

TREE FROGS

BACKGROUND

A wide variety of tree frogs live in the rain forest. While many people expect to find frogs living in the vegetation of forest floors, the tree frogs live in trees. Their feet have small padded suction cups that enable them to move from one place to another. Many of these frogs lay their eggs on leaves rather than in pools of water. When a tadpole hatches, the adult frog carries it on its back to a pool of leaf water. It is in this small pool of water that the tadpole will grow into a full-sized tree frog.

Tree frogs come in a wide variety of bright colors which serve as a warning to possible predators that the tree frogs are poisonous. In fact, the poison-dart frogs are used by indigenous peoples to create the poison for their arrows and blow darts. Color can help the tree frogs in other ways, as well. Some frogs' colors allow them to camouflage themselves well among the forest's vines and leaves. One species actually looks like a dead leaf with an almost stem-shaped nose. All of these frogs are becoming scarce as their forest habitat continues to be destroyed.

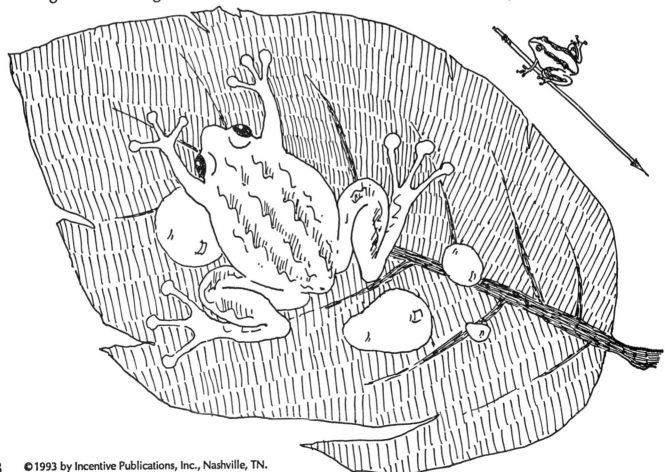

PUT ON YOUR THINKING CAP

PRIMARY   Poison-dart frogs are very colorful. If you could design a new rain forest frog, how would it look? Draw it and tell two things about it.

INTERMEDIATE   Many works of children's literature have the word "frog" in the title. List as many works of fiction (these may be children's works, or not) that you can think of with the word "frog" in the title. How many nonfiction titles can you can think of with the word "frog" in the title?

QUESTIONS WORTH RESEARCHING

PRIMARY   You now know that there are frogs in rain forests. Are there toads?

INTERMEDIATE   Compare a tree frog to an american bullfrog. In what ways are they different? In what ways are they alike? Discuss.

Tree Frog

Bull Frog

UNDERSTORY

BACKGROUND

The canopy of the rain forest blocks much of the sun's rays from the lower levels of the rain forest. These lower levels are called the "understory." Many plants that we now have in the United States, such as prayer plants and philodendron, grew originally in the rain forest understory. These plants like warm, dark places and grow well indoors. Many of the plants found in the understory have leaves that are large and flat to enable them to catch as much sunlight as possible.

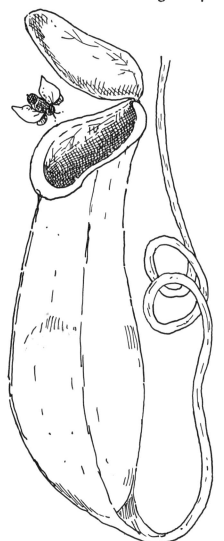

The understory is home to hundreds of thousands of interesting plants and animals. Some of the more unusual plants are those that can actually fool insects into helping them fertilize their breed by releasing a smell similar to that of decaying meat. An insect such as a beetle or fly lands on one of these flowers hoping to lay its eggs in what it believes to be decaying meat. The plant's pollen brushes against the insect as it lands on the plant. As soon as it discovers its mistake, the insect flies off only to land on another "trick" plant where it deposits the first plant's pollen.

The pitcher plant also plays a trick on unsuspecting insects. Its cup-shaped leaves look like a flower. The cup, however, is filled with water that traps and kills insects such as moths, ants, and flies. These insect victims provide the plant with nutrients necessary for the plant's survival.

The list of plants and animals found in the understory is endless. Scientists look forward to discovering and learning about many new species in the coming decades. This will only be possible if the destruction of the rain forest can be slowed or halted in the near future.

PUT ON YOUR THINKING CAP

PRIMARY   Complete the Understory Life activity.

INTERMEDIATE   There are several unusual plants like the pitcher plant in the rain forest understory; however, scientists believe there are still hundreds of thousands of plants yet to be discovered. Draw one of these undiscovered plants. Use your imagination! Describe its habitat, food source, and any other interesting features on the back of your drawing.

UNDERSTORY LIFE

Do some research to find one example each of a rain forest plant, bird, mammal, reptile, insect, and poisonous plant or animal of your choice. Write out one interesting fact and draw a picture of each one to complete the chart below.

BIRD	MAMMAL
REPTILE	INSECT
PLANT	SOMETHING POISONOUS

QUESTION WORTH RESEARCHING

PRIMARY/INTERMEDIATE   Find out what ant birds eat and how they find their food. Draw one.

VINES

BACKGROUND

Walking through a rain forest, one might notice vines hanging from the canopy and wrapping around all types of vegetation. In fact, ninety percent of all the vines in the world are found in the rain forest. These rain forest vines are called lianas. Lianas grow upward from the floor of the forest to the canopy in an attempt to reach the sunlight. Although they do not have stiff wooden trunks for support, lianas manage to move upward in one of two ways. They may wind themselves around young trees and catch a free ride as the trees grow tall, or they may wind around a large tree and climb around it to the top. To try to escape from these persistent vines, some trees have developed a slippery bark that prevents vines from entwining themselves around them.

Once they have reached the canopy layer of the forest, lianas spread in several directions, often entwining several trees together. As rain forest trees have very shallow roots, trees that are vined together create problems for one another. If one tree falls, for example, it may uproot others in the process. Some trees have actually developed a method of shedding branches which have been covered with vines so that they will not be pulled over if a nearby tree should fall.

PUT ON YOUR THINKING CAP

PRIMARY   Name as many foods as you can that grow on vines. Draw a picture of your favorite one.

INTERMEDIATE   Create some Very Vital Verse. Most of the words in the first line of these two-line verses should begin with the letter V. For example: *Vera's Volvo vroom-vrooms vitally!* Then, add a second line that features another letter: *Mighty Morris's machine moves moderately.* You may want to use themes that relate to your study of the rain forest.

QUESTIONS WORTH RESEARCHING

PRIMARY/INTERMEDIATE   Name two types of tropical vines. Draw one.

WOOD

BACKGROUND

Rain forests provide about twenty percent of all the wood used by industry worldwide. The demand for some of the beautiful hardwoods of these forests, such as teak, mahogany, and rosewood, increases each year. These woods are strong, beautiful, and resistant to insects and decay. Most homes in the United States today probably have wood from the rain forest somewhere—in furniture, wooden bowls, siding, plywood, cutting boards, or other products.

Although the United States uses a large percentage of all the wood cut from rain forests, Japan is the world's largest importer of rain forest wood. Japan imports half of all the tropical timber logged each year. Its largest logging firms are now trying to expand their harvest of tropical woods into the Amazon rain forests. Logging can greatly affect a forest region. For example, the sale of prized woods such as mahogany and ebony has caused the virtual disappearance of the rain forests from Mexico.

PUT ON YOUR THINKING CAP

PRIMARY   Read Shel Silverstein's book *The Giving Tree* (Harper & Row, 1964). If trees really had feelings, how would the last mahogany tree of the Mexican rain forest feel about its life? Draw the tree below and write a story about it.

INTERMEDIATE   While much of the hardwood harvested from rain forests is made into beautiful furniture or wood for homes, some of it is used for such items as cardboard boxes and paper. Create a television advertisement that will alert consumers to this fact. How can we be sure that the stores we do business with are not contributing to the loss of the rain forest? Use the Reporter's Triangle to help you structure an impressive commercial to persuade companies to stop using rain forest wood in their products.

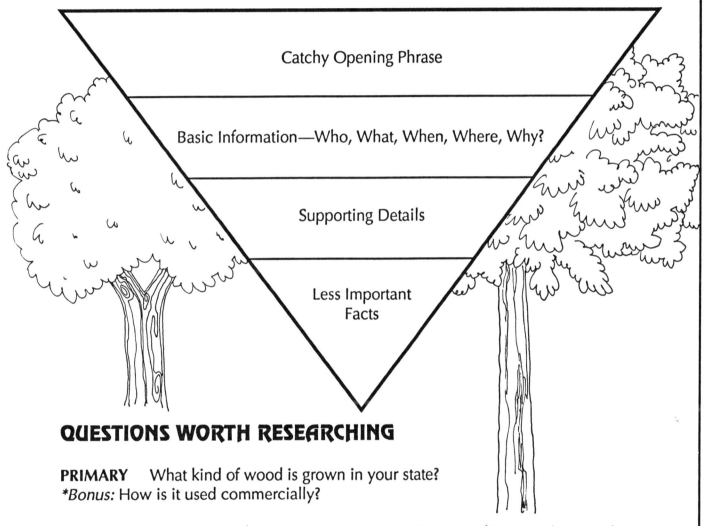

Catchy Opening Phrase

Basic Information—Who, What, When, Where, Why?

Supporting Details

Less Important Facts

QUESTIONS WORTH RESEARCHING

PRIMARY   What kind of wood is grown in your state?
Bonus: How is it used commercially?

INTERMEDIATE   Research your way into an acrostic poem. (An acrostic poem is one in which the first letters of each line form a word.) To begin, use the name of a type of wood, and write one fact for each letter.

Ebony is a black wood.
Black bark covers ebony's white sapwood.
Only in India and Sri Lanka will you find
New ebony trees—so please be kind!
(You may also find this wood on your piano keys!)

XINGU RIVER

BACKGROUND

The Xingu River is a major tributary of the Amazon River and courses through the rain forest of Brazil. Many of the Indian peoples who live on the banks of the Xingu River are concerned about the preservation of their culture. The Kayapo, a tribe that lives in Central Brazil, farm the land along the Xingu and fish as they have done for hundreds of years. The government of Brazil has recently proposed to develop the area by building a series of electricity-producing dams along the Xingu. Not only will this development ruin the Kayapo's hunting grounds, but outsiders carry diseases that are foreign to the immune systems of the natives. The Indians who come in contact with these foreign diseases often become ill and die.

In 1988, Indians of the Xingu River area met with leaders of the World Bank in Washington, D.C. to protest the building of the dams. Brazil's government had asked The World Bank for a loan to fund the project. As a result of the meeting, the building of one of the dams has been cancelled. The Kayapo and other Indian groups continue to fight for the preservation of their traditional way of life.

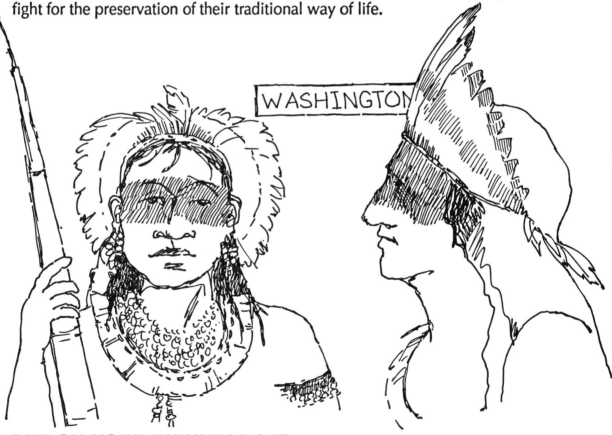

PUT ON YOUR THINKING CAP

INTERMEDIATE   Research to find the name of a river that begins with each letter of the alphabet, if possible. You already have the letter X covered! List the rivers in alphabetical order and give the location of each. Then, see if you can find them on a map or globe.

PRIMARY   Problem-Solving: The Indians of the Xingu River basin have a problem that they are working to solve. Use the Problem-Solving Grid to help you brainstorm and evaluate the following problem: Students continue to run in the hallway at school even though they have been repeatedly warned not to run. The teachers are afraid someone will be hurt.

PROBLEM-SOLVING GRID

Possible Solutions	Must Be Safe	Must Be Fair	Must Be Cheap	Must Be Enforceable	Score
Score each item: 3=good 2=fair 1=poor					

QUESTIONS WORTH RESEARCHING

PRIMARY/INTERMEDIATE   Draw a picture of a hydroelectric dam and one of a beaver dam. Are the two dams alike in any way?

YAGUA INDIANS

BACKGROUND

The Yagua Indians of the South American rain forest live completely off the land, leaving or creating almost no pollution. They make their clothing primarily from dried grasses and leaves and hunt their food in the forest canopy. In order to hunt effectively, they create poisonous arrows and blow darts as weapons. The poison they use is extracted from the region's poisonous tree frogs. The Yagua dip their arrows and darts into the poison, and when they shoot an animal such as a monkey or bird the paralyzing poison causes the animal to lose its grip on a tree branch and fall to the ground. In addition to hunting, the Yagua are also gardeners. They grow fruits such as pineapples, bananas, and sugarcane.

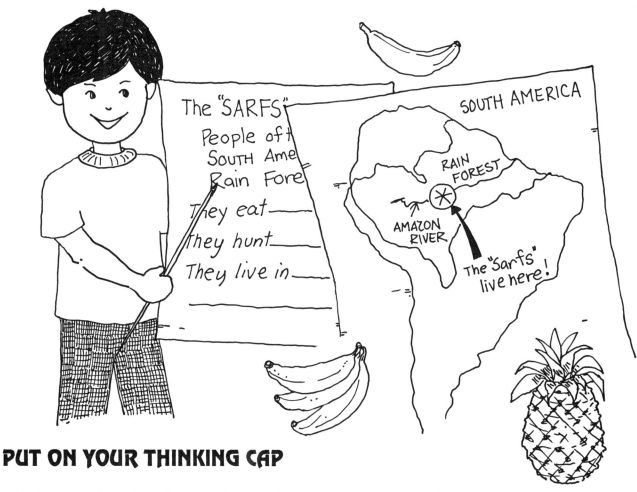

PUT ON YOUR THINKING CAP

PRIMARY   Complete the Rain Forest Rhymes activity (page 59).

INTERMEDIATE   To us, Yagua seems an unusual name for a group of people. Create a name for a recently discovered culture found only in a remote area of the Amazon rain forest. Describe this culture in detail. What do they eat? How do they hunt? How many people live in one tribe? What types of homes do they live in? Draw pictures of the people and of one other interesting aspect of their culture.

QUESTIONS WORTH RESEARCHING

PRIMARY   Find out what kinds of frogs are poisonous. Draw a picture of one type of poisonous frog and label it.

INTERMEDIATE   Compare the modern-day Yagua culture to an American Indian culture of the 19th century. Discuss their similarities and differences.

RAIN FOREST RHYMES

Read the words in each line. Circle the ones that rhyme. Then, circle the letter that shows the total number of rhyming words for the row. These letters will form a secret phrase. Write it on the line below.

					2	3	4
1.	rain	gain	plane	queen	S	Y	L
2.	seed	read	field	key	A	M	R
3.	dart	cart	bird	snort	G	T	C
4.	frog	fog	rag	mad	U	L	O
5.	tree	flea	free	me	P	W	A
6.	plant	ant	can't	brat	F	I	V
7.	fruit	groove	flute	rude	N	B	A
8.	food	good	mood	sued	E	D	G
9.	bird	word	tired	him	I	W	R
10.	big	fig	jig	dig	V	S	A
11.	small	call	will	crawl	R	N	H

Answer Key, page 63

Z ZAIRE

BACKGROUND

Zaire is a country located in central Africa. In the Congo River basin of Zaire, isolated bands of native peoples live in much the same way as their ancestors did thousands of years ago. A large undisturbed part of what is left of the world's rain forests can also be found in Zaire. One region of this forest is known as the Ituri Forest and is occupied by people of short stature sometimes referred to as pygmies, although these people prefer to be known by their tribal names rather than the broad reference of pygmy. (Pygmy simply means short.) Three of the largest tribes found in the Ituri Forest are the Baka, the Efe, and the Mbuti.

These natives of Zaire use the plants and the animals of the forest to provide their daily needs. From over 100 varieties of plants, they create medicines, clothes, baskets, shelter, and meals. They live simply, moving from place to place in search of food.

AFRICA

CONGO RIVER

ZAIRE

Dear Fr...

PUT ON YOUR THINKING CAP

PRIMARY Write a letter to an imaginary child in the Ituri forest of Zaire. Describe your daily routine. How will you explain your school to your new pen pal?

INTERMEDIATE   Create a six-page "Fact vs. Fiction Book." On pages 1, 3, and 5 of your book write a statement about the rain forest of Zaire that appears factual, but may or may not be true. Illustrate each statement. On pages 2, 4, and 6 explain whether the statement on the preceding page is true or not. Illustrate your explanations.

QUESTION WORTH RESEARCHING

PRIMARY/INTERMEDIATE   Choose another word relating to the rain forest that begins with the letter Z. Research to find out three facts about it.

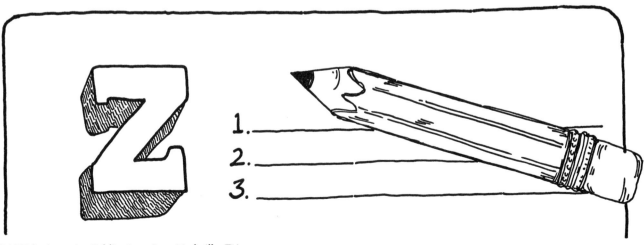

ANSWER KEYS

Animal Card Riddles, page 9

1. Flying Fox
2. Tarsier
3. Ocelot
4. Gorilla
5. Sloth
6. Civet
7. Potto
8. Tree Kangaroo

Word Find, page 39

					A											
G				E	M	E	R	G	E	N	T			H		
O				Q	A	R	A	F	F	L	E	S	I	A		
R				U	Z									B		
F				A	O									I	H	
E				T	N	C	A	N	O	P	Y		N	T		
E				O								A	O	A		
R		P	E	R	I	W	I	N	K	L	E	C	L	T		
T												U	S	S		
								O								
					Y	R	O	T	S	R	E	D	N	U		
	D	E	F	O	R	E	S	T	A	T	I	O	N			

Tribal Messages, page 41

The forest's peoples live in warm jungle areas and under the forest's canopy. (The tribes are: EFE, KAYAPO, BAKA, SENOI, NEGRITO, BAMBUTI, MBUTI, WAURA.)

Alphabet Mystery, page 43

Songbirds

Anagram Puzzle, page 45

1. Tax
2. Batter
3. Start
4. Brute
5. Trust
6. Street
7. Utter
8. Steal
9. Texas
10. Brat

Rain Forest Rhymes, page 59

Yagua Indian

A Recycling Message

If the time should arrive that this book has outlasted its classroom usefulness, you may continue its cycle as a recyclable product by:

- Taking its pages to your recycling center
- Reusing the cover as a file folder, or cutting it up to make colorful game markers, bookmarks, manipulative teaching aids, or alphabet cutouts for bulletin board displays